MW01289288

Love Letters

PART I: DEDICATED TO THE LOST ART OF COMMUNICATION

STAN PEARSON II
JOHNNY REYNOLDS

Copyright © 2009 by Stan Pearson II and Johnny Reynolds

All rights reserved. No part of this book may be reproduced in any form or by any electronic or mechanical means, including information storage and retrieval systems, without the permission in writing from the author, except by a reviewer who may quote brief passages in a review.

First Edition: 2009

Cover Designs and Layout by Abra Johnson, AbraJohnson@Mac.com
Editing by Kristin Walinski, www.ScribeOnDemand.com

Love Letters/ Stan Pearson II, Johnny Reynolds

Further information on this book
and the work of
Stan Pearson II
and Johnny Reynolds
available at:

www.StanPearson.com
www.TheArtOfLoveLetters.com

Introduction

This movement is dedicated to the Art of expression, the Soul of the Mind, and the Pulse that keeps the heart beating.

This book will take you to places you have once been and want to return to again. We hope to take you to that part of yourself you thought you lost—we hope to help you find it. We will give you the voice you thought went unheard—now it will be impossible to ignore. This book is dedicated to love lost, love found, and love you didn't even know existed.

We have partnered in this work because love is something misunderstood and misrepresented. We believe the key to love is communication. In the midst of the era of text messaging and voicemail, we have lost the ability to express our thoughts in a complete form. This loss even affects young people in their classes, because they as well as adults learn to communicate through abbreviations. We have thus cheated words, ourselves, and relationships.

Communication is what puts us on solid ground in any relationship. This volume's focus on communication will do exactly that. We hope it will jump start your return to communicating in a form that will serve as therapy and fresh air.

Please enjoy and take advantage of this opportunity to express yourself.

Welcome to love letters.

Have you ever felt
like you needed to ask
Love a few questions?

I did.

Instead of keeping everything inside, I wrote a letter . . .

Hey Love,

Last night as I watched you sleep, I thought to myself, are you dreaming about me? I wondered, does your mind take you to the same places you seem to take me when you're awake?

You have taken me to my highest point and my lowest, but I guess that's what this love thing is all about. The adventures we have embarked on together have been quite the roller coaster ride, but I wouldn't trade our experiences for world.

Last night as I watched you sleep, I asked myself, are we on the same page? Because every time I think I've got you figured out, you throw me for a loop. Why is that when I want to walk away, I can't? When I want to give up, you won't let me? Do you get a kick out of all of this?

Tell me how it is possible for you to make me feel so good, yet hurt me so badly. Tell me how you can make me feel so strong, yet feel so weak at the same time. I know there is a method to your madness—or am I the one who's mad?

Last night as I watched you sleep, I couldn't help but wonder why you do the things you do. Is it all just a game to you?

Wait! I think I got it: you want to keep me guessing so I can dream just like you, right? If I stop dreaming, I stop loving, because to love is to dream.

Love in itself is a dream coming true. Now I understand why I wrote this letter and where you are coming from. And to think it took you falling asleep for me to get the point.

Could you do me a favor? The next you want to make a point, please don't keep me up all night.

Sincerely,
Thinking of You

I tried to tell her what I
was feeling, but I knew it would lead to an argument.

So I wrote a letter . . .

Girl, you sure know how to work a nerve.

Do you always start your day with an attitude? I'm writing you because I know if I were to talk to you, it would lead to a shouting match, and today just ain't the day.

You think you know what's going on, but you really don't. Just because you've dated some men who didn't do right by you, don't hold their mistakes against me.

I'm not the type of guy who bites his tongue or who has a problem expressing himself. Maybe that's why we are at this point now. I know I'm not the easiest person in the world to be in a relationship with, but I'm an honest man. When I love, I love hard.

I give you my best even when you make me think it's just not good enough. What happened to us? Somewhere along the line, you stopped trusting me, and I know I didn't give you a reason to.

Have you been watching too much TV? Let me guess. You've been listening to your girlfriends who don't have the slightest idea how to make relationships work. If I say, "I will call you back," give me a chance to do so before you attempt to call me again. If I say, "I'm at work" when you call, understand it's not that I don't want to talk to you—it's because I am busy making a living for you,. If I say I'm going out with my boys, trust I'm coming home to you, and only you.

Girl, I'm starting to feel like I'm wearing a turtleneck in the summertime! Just let me breathe. I'm not going anywhere. I'm in this for the long haul, and you used to know that.

Are we destined to be one of those "break up to make up" scenarios? God, I hope not!

The purpose of this letter is not to point fingers, but to help us get back to the basics, as they say. Sure, the easy thing to do is to just walk away, but I'm trying to prove I'm not like those other men. I hope after reading this you will feel better about where we stand so we can actually talk without all the yelling.

Sincerely,
Free your mind

It had been a while
since I had spoken to the Heavenly Father.

I wanted to reach out to thank
Him or something.

Have you ever felt like you
needed a one-on-one?

I did the best I could,
and it is in this letter . . .

I do apologize for not sitting down and taking the time to write this sooner. You made everything possible. You faced all of the struggle, the hardship, and the ridicule just for me. If I am going to be honest with myself, I have to say I don't know if I would have done the same. Truthfully, I don't know if I would have been strong enough to do the same.

There are times when I look up and thank you, but a thank you isn't always enough. There's nothing like being able to jot your feelings down as they come with no censor or hesitation in thought. I am glad I finally took the time.

Maybe this is a little selfish, but I feel better with every word that evolves from my head and trickles down to my fingertips. Remember when I was walking with that huge group, and you told me I shouldn't be there? I already knew that, but you just had to reassure me, and I made a swift beeline for the alley and went right back to the family room floor. It could have been me that came back hurt.

Remember when I thought I was alone crying as I sat in the kitchen, thousands of miles away from my family? You were right there, and I wasn't alone. My tears dried and I turned on some music and had the best one-person party. I don't know how you did it, but you did. You do it for everyone. We don't always see it, but it's there.

I know this got to be a little bit long, but it was overdue. I am smiling as I write because you've been good to me. You teach me lessons, and if I'm listening closely enough, I get it.

Thank you for everything, and I'll keep on pushing as best as I can. I'll try to keep in better contact. You're the best!

Sincerely,
God's Child

I felt like I was losing hope,
and the only way to feel
better was to express
my hope of finding
my Nubian King.

It was important
that I took this time to
write a short letter . . .

I gave up hope on finding a strong Black Man, because the notion of a Black Man who is sensitive and caring and who will pay attention to my needs seems quite impossible.

The chances of finding a good Black Man are always low. Black men have the highest rate of being incarcerated and the lowest rate of high school graduation. The list can go on and on.

Just once, I want to find a Black Man who is successful. My Black Man doesn't necessarily have to have a degree, but he has to have a business plan and be emotional and spiritual. When I say emotional, I mean he knows how to kiss, make love, and hold hands in public. He must also have a sense of spirituality—he can't be afraid to read the Word and pray for a solution.

He must appreciate dating a pretty woman with intelligence. Yes, some men have told me I'm too pretty and I would get too much attention. Also, some have told me I am too opinionated, but I don't plan on changing that quality to fit anyone's agenda.

My question is, are there any available Black Men?

Is Cliff Huxtable just a character on television?

Is Will Smith just for Jada?
At 26, will God bless me with a strong Black Man I can love?

I do believe in the concepts of soul mates and marriage.

When will I be blessed?

Sincerely,
Waiting Patiently

A letter dedicated to
my love . . .

I walked a thousand miles to meet you.
It feels like I took only a few steps, and then you appeared.
When I gaze in your eyes,
I've found the light missing in my dark world.
I used to think I would never find you.
However, something so deep inside of me
reassured me you would come along.
I use to think Fate and Faith were for celebrities,
but now I know they're for
common folks like me, too.
Am I dreaming I met my guy?
Are you hungry?
How can I please you?
Are you real?
I thank my lucky stars for a man like you.

Thank you.

*Sometimes you have a feeling or experience
that can only be explained through
your words.*

This is one of those times . . .

Dear Poetry,

I remember when we first met like it was yesterday. I was just walking around the store, minding my own business—browsing, not really looking for anything. I was just enjoying the ambiance of the store, and then there you were.

I slowly walked by, admiring your cover—everything from the design, to the lettering, to the color. I remember thinking the binding holding your pages together was like nothing I had ever seen before. I took a minute to catch my breath. I thought, this is just another book—why am I tripping? I continued to walk around the store. There must have been a sale or something because you were everywhere. Now, I must admit, I was enjoying the view.

After crossing paths a couple times, one had to wonder what was inside. Or shall I say, I wondered what was inside. Something about you had intrigued me. Without saying anything, you had me.

Soon after came the introduction. You know, it's funny: when you are introduced to something for the first time, it takes you a minute to take it all in. Well, that's if you are interested in more than just the average book. Yeah, your cover looked nice, but what made you any different than the book right next to you on the shelf? I couldn't put my finger on it, but there was something different about you.

I had heard people talk about their experiences when they were introduced to poetry for the first time, and with this weird but pleasant tingling inside, I decided to take a deeper look. As I read the brief description on your back, I desired to experience poetry more and more. Wow, I thought to myself, where did this come from? It was the most amazing first encounter I had ever had. It's funny how the little things touch you the most. As I experienced more and more of you, I was drawn closer and closer to you. I couldn't even remember what I came to the store for. I had actually come to the mall with no intentions on coming in the bookstore.

Was this fate?

I hadn't even gotten past the table of contents, and I had already fallen for you. I was so caught up in the essence of you that I lost track of time. Was it really midnight? It was as if I weren't even in the store. It was just you and me and the aroma of coffee. Then that darn voice over the loud speaker had to interrupt what had been such a sweet encounter of intimacy to announce that the store would be closing in ten minutes. I had no idea if I would ever be able to fully experience you, but I desired to. I tried not to let on how much I wanted you, as if it weren't noticeable that every time you came near me, my temperature rose.

I thought about you, and I just had to write you to let you know I am so glad I was able to experience what makes you you, and share with you the inner pieces of me. At times it seems as if we are one and the same. After finishing a piece, I think to myself, now, did I write that or did you? It is like our thoughts are one and the same. I can share anything and everything with you, and you can share anything with me. I read and then write; all it takes is just a book, paper, and a pen. That's all we started with, and it's all we will ever need.

Poetry, you hold a very special place in my heart.

Wow, you are just my first collection, and I am enjoying every page. I look forward to wherever this journey may lead us.

Love,
Essence

*Every day I feel like I
have met the person of
my dreams and it drives me crazy because I don't know
who she is supposed to be.*

*I wasn't sure how to bring
up this conversation
with a friend, so I decided
to write a letter . . .*

It happened again.

How am I supposed to deal with this? If I meet one more incredible woman, I think I'll back up and run full speed into the first brick wall I see. No, better yet, I'll walk barefoot across a gravel road as I kick rocks.

How does this happen? What happens when you meet one great woman or man right after another? You almost feel stuck. Options are good to have, but once you have those options, how are you supposed to make that all-important decision? You walk down the street, shop in a mall, or simply go to church, and there he or she is, the person of your dreams, only to find out that beautiful and intelligent people are everywhere.

I'm writing because I needed to get this out. I think I have the entire dating scene down. I know exactly what I want and how I want it, until I get it. Then boom!, the qualifications shift.

Maybe it is my confidence or charm, but it seems as though women fall out of the sky sometimes. Sometimes I think life would be easier if terrible women were attracted to me, but that is hardly the case. If I could only be approached by the woman chewing with her mouth open, zero table manners, and no goals or aspirations. I suppose that would make things easier, but then I'd have something else to complain about. Options are blessings, and I won't take them for granted.

I suppose at this point, I have to be more honest with myself than anyone else. What kind of woman is supposed to be the Mrs.? What woman can I bring out the best in, and vice-versa? That becomes the question. That's easier said than done, but it is an issue to be dealt with nonetheless.

Sometimes the song "Beautiful Women" by BoyzIIMen screams in my head as theme music, but that's not who I want to be. I want to be everything to my one and only. Quite honestly, I think my experiences meeting these great women are letting me know exactly what I want in my Queen. The good, the bad, and the ugly are realities, and I need to know what percentage of each of them I can live with.

Okay, I get it now. I need, want, and will respect these experiences and these women. They are keys to my future, so I need to pay close attention. They see in me what I should always see in myself, and I see in them what my dream is for always.

Truly,
Eligible Bachelor

*I had to tell you ladies something, whether
you agree or not.*

*I don't know everything,
but I wanted to share
the little I do know.*

*The best way was to put
it into this letter . . .*

Quite honestly ladies, I'll tell you this: you don't need to tell me you're not like other girls or that you live a drama-free life, because I know you're lying. Yes, I'm talking to you! I love all of you to death, but there's no such thing as a drama-free woman.

I'll tell you this: we men don't appreciate being treated like we are not intelligent creatures. Some of us are very intelligent, and we see through your act.

I'll tell you this: you don't have to do anything earth-shattering to get our attention. The more you are who you are, the more we are drawn to you. The more you act like someone you are not, the more you will attract someone who is doing the same thing.

I'll tell you this: every man who wants to buy you a drink is not going to be a pain. Remember this: if you accept the drink, you accept the consequence. There may be something to be said for a guy who offers to buy you a coke, lemonade, or water. He may be smooth, but acknowledge the creativity. At least that guy might be a little more fun to talk to. Again, if you accept the drink, you accept the consequence. While it sounds heavy, it's the truth.

I'll tell you this: keep an eye on the hater friend. She hates for a reason, and it is not always in your best interest. I know she's your friend, but everyone has an angle. Remember that. Try not to be the woman who hears a terrible story and then comes back to take it out on her man. That's classic.

I'll tell you this: a beautiful woman is not the one who hears it all day or who responds to the calls and whistles. A beautiful woman is the one who knows she's beautiful without the approval of others. She walks tall and sure in the face of doubt and distress. That is the kind of woman that attracts a good man.

Always,
I'll Tell You This

I couldn't believe
our first encounter
resulted in all of this.

I never explained it
to you from my point of view, so I wrote a letter to you.

You know how I am
about this kind of stuff.

I hope it makes sense . . .

How do I put this? I didn't know what to think initially. I was invited to this get-together, and normally I decline, but for some reason I went for it this time. I rang the doorbell, and a friend of yours answered it with a warm greeting. I greeted those who I knew already, introduced myself to strangers, and proceeded into the kitchen where you were.

You turned around with a smile, as if you already knew who I was going to be in your future. It seemed like just another everyday encounter, and maybe that's how it snuck up on me. The encounter was like dropping a seed in the earth without realizing its potential. We laughed, we joked, and we flirted. Who would have known I was supposed to be there to meet a friend of yours? Whoops!

The signals had already been sent, the smiles had already been exchanged. The evening was filled with great food and great company. Stop smiling at me! I'm cool and suave. I smile on my own terms.

You were inviting, you were fun, and you were who you were supposed to be. This is what it is supposed to be like. So what now? You have no clue I'm thinking about all of these things. At least I've come to grips with the fact I have these thoughts. Maybe I'll let you know someday.

Sincerely,
First Impression

*Have you ever just
wanted to go bananas?*

*I have wanted to go
completely crazy
for a few reasons.*

One of them is crazy drivers.

*You know exactly
what I mean too.*

*Writing a letter was safer
than saying what I wanted to say out loud, so here it is . . . .*

Where in the world are you going? I cannot stand this. If one more person . . .

Hey you jerk, if I wasn't with my mom—

Excuse me, pardon me, where did they learn how to move like that? I would slap somebody if that happened to me again. I can't believe this happens to me every time I go out.

It doesn't matter how careful I am, some idiot has to appear and ruin something!

What is your purpose in life? I just need to calm down and take a deep breath.

I'd be a little better if I said a prayer or two. You are getting on my last good nerve.

I can't do this. On top of everything else, I won't be able to get by, let alone be where I'm supposed to be when I'm supposed to be there.

God, help me and the person I'm dealing with if something bad happens.

That's right! Okay, I'm breathing again. Thanks, because sometimes I just feel like I'm losing it.

Truly,
Road Rage

*Ladies, we don't always mean
to be total imbeciles or
insensitive to your needs.*

*Sometimes, we are just brain
dead or terribly scared.*

*Trust me, that part of it
is harder on us than it is you.*

*There are many times we
exhibit this bad behavior, but
I had to write you a letter
about one of them . . .*

What do you mean you're having a baby?
Are you sure?
What day is it?
When is the last time you checked?
Did you go to the doctor?
Did you ask your mother?
Did she dream of fish?
We were standing up, weren't we?
I thought you said we were going to wait.
What about the responsibility?
What am I supposed to do?
Alright, so . . . is it mine?
What do you mean, how can I ask?
When is your due date?
Did you tell your girlfriend?
What did she say?
And your mom, how did she say it?
What about the dog and the three tropical fish we just

bought?
Did your father pass out?
Was he happy?
Does he want to sit down with me and have the talk? He's
going to kill me, isn't he?
Did you see that episode of Grey's Anatomy?
What can I do to help?
What do you need me to do?
We're in this together, right?
Do you think I can handle it like you can?
Do you think I have what it takes to be great dad?

Sincerely,
Scared Poppa

I am confused and I don't quite understand something, so I decided to write a letter....

Hey, how are you?

I see you're just getting home from a lovely evening, and I bet you're all excited about that first date huh?

You spent a lot of time picking out your clothes, making sure you looked your best. You even made sure you arrived a few minutes early because you know you only get one chance to make a first impression.

You opened every door for her, and you even pulled out her chair. Your conversation was on point, and you made sure not to say anything stupid that would turn her off.

Way to go!

I don't even have to ask, but I know you loved that goodnight kiss she gave you. You didn't even have to go for it because she came to you. Nice work!

Now what if I told you that tomorrow, she won't call you, and all the excitement you feel right now will be for nothing?

What if I said that if you sent her a text message to say "Good morning pretty lady," she wouldn't even take the time to respond?

You just had the ideal first date, and the next day, it will seem like nothing ever happened.

Women are something else, aren't they? But that's the joy of dating—you win some and you lose some.

Don't worry though—she'll call you the day after tomorrow.

Sincerely,
Chival-why?

I asked myself, is honesty really the best policy?

My mind started to wonder . . .
so I decided to write a letter . . .

Why couldn't you just tell me you were seeing someone else? Did you think I wasn't strong enough to handle the truth?

Or is it that you were trying to decide whether or not you were going to attempt to get away with living a double life? We talked every day, and when we met, I believe I asked you if you were dating anyone. I even went so far as to make it easy for you by joking, "okay, at least tell me what my competition is going to be like."

Come on, we are no longer living in the olden days where people have to tiptoe around the subject of dating multiple people or even playing the field. I can understand that. My point is, be honest and up front and respect me enough to let me decide whether I want to stick around or not.

To find out in this fashion that everything I thought I knew about you is a lie and that you are actually the complete opposite of the person you portrayed yourself to be is shocking. How do you think that makes me feel? I get it, it's not really about my feelings though, it's about you "having your cake and eating it too" as they say. Well, I hope it was delicious.

I guess I'll let you go now, because I'm sure you have to get back to your "real life." Sorry to have bothered you.

Love,
Second Choice

PS: I guess I should say congratulations, I hear you're expecting a baby.

Sometimes we wait years to apologize to a loved one,
but I didn't want to wait any longer
so I wrote him a letter.

My son, I know we haven't had the best relationship in the past but there's something I feel I need to tell you. Although our situation isn't a unique one, it's one that definitely needs to be addressed. You see I blame myself for not being there when you needed me the most and I know no matter how much I say it , a thousand sorries could never make up for all the things I've missed.

I've seen the pictures and read the articles but I still feel a sense of emptiness inside. There isn't a day that goes by that I don't question my actions. Why couldn't I have been stronger? Was it worth it? And Will I ever gain your trust?

It's been ten long years since I've left. And while I know you don't need me to tell you this, you've become quite the young man; tall, dark, and handsome. You've managed to accomplish so much in such a short period time.

Son words cannot even express how proud I am of you. And to top it all off, you've been able to accomplish all of this while becoming a father yourself. And in closing I leave you with this:

Son, I'm sorry for not being there when you went through puberty and when you got your first kiss.

I'm sorry for not being there to give you the guidance and emotional support.

I'm sorry for not being there to tell you all about the birds and the bees.

And more importantly, I'm sorry for not being there when you needed me the most.

Asking for your Forgiveness...

Your Father

I was too embarrassed to
tell anyone this,
so I wrote a letter instead . . .

I'm so glad I caught you; I'm shocked you're even up this late. Usually when I say something to you, I have to wait until the next day for you to finally respond.

I find myself anticipating your responses and hanging on your every word. Am I crazy?

Do you talk to everyone like this? Or is it that you're bored, and going back and forth with me all this time gives you something to do?

You might be too good to be true. You're extremely attractive from what I've seen so far, you seem to have a great personality, you say all the right things, and you laugh at all my jokes, even when I don't think they're that funny.

Okay, something's got to be wrong with you. Is this even really you?

I'm glad you made me "a friend," and I look forward to the next time we are able to chat. I guess I am about to log off now, because we both should be asleep anyway. Look at us, acting like we don't have to go to work in the morning.

Be good, and I'll catch you next time, okay?

Until then . . .

Oh, by the way, do you think we should actually meet?

Sincerely,
Computer Love

*I just don't think I
should talk about this,
so instead I'm
writing a letter . . .*

I think I'm addicted to women. There is nothing like a beautiful woman. Now, I don't just mean a pretty face and hot body. I mean the essence of a woman.

Sure, women can be moody, and they are probably one of the most sensitive things God has ever created. Each one comes with an internal stamp that says "handle with care."

Is there anything that can drive a man crazier than a woman?

Let's just be honest: half the things we do as men, we do because we want to impress or gain the interest of women.

For instance, I have a friend who gets his hair cut and his face shaved three days a week. Sure, he wants to look good for himself, but what he is really doing is making sure he is always at his best just in case he meets a beautiful woman.

And the wonderful thing about a beautiful woman is you can almost see one anywhere. At the mall, in the grocery store, on the job—the list goes on and on.

There is nothing more powerful than a beautiful woman. A woman can say something to you or touch you in such a way that changes your life forever. She can make you feel like you're sitting on top of the world. I don't know about you, but to me, that's power.

So I wrote this letter to help cope with my addiction, because I don't think talking to someone in a therapy session would help. If there is a cure for this, I don't think I want it, because I don't mind being hooked on this thing called a beautiful woman.

*She asked me
to be her "little secret."*

*I couldn't talk to anyone,
so I wrote a letter instead . . .*

Hey there,

I hope you had a good day today, especially since I know it bothered you that you couldn't talk to me. But I guess that's how you want it since you are too scared to step outside the comfort zone you have made for yourself.

You're not in love, and you probably don't have a clue what love is.

You wanted to spend time with me despite the fact that you're in a "relationship" with someone else.

I'm writing this letter because you wanted to keep me as your "little secret," but I don't think that's going to work for me. What you are asking is for me to put on blinders. You want me to disregard the fact that when you leave me, you go home to someone else. You want me to believe the things you say to me aren't the same things you turn around and say to him.

I'll admit, for a moment I thought about playing this dangerous game with you, but I don't want to block my future blessings by disrespecting another man.

Sure, I don't know him, and we'll probably never meet. But that also raises the question of would you do the same thing to me?

You say you're not as happy as you want to be, but because you've invested time in that relationship, you don't want to walk away.

Now how much sense does that make? Don't you know that this is your life, and you only have one to live?

Let's just say someone offered you your dream house,

dream car, and dream job.

Would you take it? Or would you continue to pay rent, take the bus, and punch the clock and watch your life pass you by?

Life is about choices and living with the consequences of those choices. So I'll end this letter on a goodbye note, and I'll apologize in advance . . . because I know when you're with him you're thinking about me. Sorry about that.

Love,
Little Secret

Before I let the cat
out of the bag,
let me jot down
my thoughts
in this letter . . .

What type of woman do I really want? Let's be honest, we all have a "type." We all know what we like and don't like, what turns us on, and—definitely—what turns us off.

Do I want the Supermodel or the Superwoman? Am I looking for the Homerun or the Homemaker? Some people spend their whole lives searching for what they think they want, only to find out they really have no clue what that is.

Is it more important for a woman to be pretty or sexy? Every woman has the potential to be pretty, but not every woman can be sexy. Cause to me, pretty is a dime a dozen, but sexy makes a man come home at night.

If she loves to cook and clean, does that mean she won't get down and dirty if necessary?

If she is more of a homebody, will she trip when I want to go out and party?

I'm writing this letter because I need some clarity on what I really want in a mate.

I wanted to be excited beyond measure about a woman. When I see her number come across my phone, I want to feel like I can't pick up the phone fast enough because I know it's her.

When I know I'm about to see her, I want to feel like I can't sit still because I'm anticipating her arrival.

I want every date to feel like it's the first. Is this even possible, or do I want the fairy tale?

Is it possible to live the American Dream with the perfect wife, home, white picket fence, two kids, and a dog?

Is there such a thing as the "total package"? Or will the dream ultimately lead to total disappointment? I can't afford to get this wrong, because no one wants to be alone forever.

And let's not forget, every King needs a Queen.

I want to get something
off my chest about women who always have an
excuse for everything.
They have excuses for the small stuff too.
Are they credible?

Who knows, so I put my thoughts in a letter . . .

Hey,

Don't you hate it when people use excuses? Those people who claim to be "too busy" all the time, or those who say "something just came up at the last minute." People make time for the things they want to make time for, no matter how busy they are. So when people say they are "too busy," what they're really saying is they're too busy for you.

I'm sure I'm not the only person who has reached out to someone who always says what they "meant" to do— "Oh, I meant to call you back."

It takes about 2.5 seconds to pick up your phone and say "hi," even if you only have a second to talk before you have to go. I'd rather get a little bit of effort from someone than get a whole lot of nothing.

I'm a busy person too. Everyone who is living this thing called life can find themselves busy. So if I can find the time to get back to people, they can surely find the time to get back to me.

I just can't do excuses anymore. I think we let too many things slide because of them, and it's time out for that.

Just wanted to get that off my chest real quick and I do feel a lot better . . . so thank you.

Love,
Frustration

*I really don't
know what to say,
so I decided to
write this letter . . .*

Dear Ms. Unknown,

I'm writing you because I didn't want to offend you in conversation. I'm almost at a loss for words because I've never been in a situation like this. I've heard stories about men who have attempted to deal with situations like this, but I don't know of any actual success stories. When we started talking to each other, there seemed to be an instant vibe there, a chemistry if you will. I loved your smile, and it grabbed my attention from the first "hello." We exchanged pleasantries for hours before I decided to ask the simple question "so, what do you do for a living?" I'm not sure why it took me so long to ask something so basic; maybe I was distracted by your effortless beauty and great personality. Nonetheless, when you told me you were a "dancer," I paused. In the back of my mind, I thought please don't mean "dancer" in the since of late night, sliding down a pole, with money in the air dancing—anything but that!

Then you proceeded to tell me that yes, you are an exotic dancer, and that what you really do for a living is "sell dreams." I thought it was pretty funny when you said that because you had been selling me a dream for the last couple hours and you didn't even know it.

Why couldn't you say you were a teacher, a lawyer, a police officer, or even a waitress? A stripper! I don't know how I feel about that. Am I progressive enough to handle the fact that this is your chosen hustle? Can I deal with the fact that if we were to start dating one another, any random man can come to a place and see what you have to offer anytime he wants?

Yeah, as men, we laugh and joke all the time about what we would do if we met a woman you liked and she told you she was a stripper? What would you do if you were me and the tables were turned? Could I really take you home to my mother, who inevitably will ask, "what is it that you do?" Do you really think you will be able to get away with the response, "I sell dreams?" No way—not in this lifetime!

So I'm writing this letter because I'm stuck between a rock and a hard place. You do seem like a very sweet woman with a lot to offer someone, and it has been my pleasure thus far to have met you. But the question is— does it begin and end here? I just don't know if I'll ever be comfortable enough with what you do. I don't know if this letter helped the situation or made it worse, but maybe we can talk about it later. Until then, you be careful.

Sincerely,
Judgmental

I didn't want her to
find out until it was time,

so I put my thoughts in this letter . . .

Man I've got to get this right, everything has to be perfect. I mean, she's been waiting for this moment her whole life.

As a little girl, she dreamed of how she would like this moment to go, and today I will make her dream come true. I want her to remember this forever. I mean, other guys may have done this differently, but I want to set the bar so high she feels likes she's floating on cloud nine.

Sure, it might have taken me a while to know I wanted to do this or to build up the courage to do this, but I am 200% sure that now is the time. Her family is behind me: I have their love and support, so today is the day.

Okay. Let me go over the list of things one more time. Okay, looks good; okay, check; okay, that's right.

I love her, she's the one. I can't breathe without her. Okay, yeah, I'm ready.

I can't wait to see her expression; I know she is going to be surprised.

Here she comes. All right, it's showtime!

Love,
Marriage Proposal

*I had some things I wanted to express
to myself, so I started writing.*

This is what I came up with . . .

Hey you,

I see you're really starting to come into your own. A lot of your dreams are becoming reality, and it's making me smile.

You've come a long way from that clumsy, shy guy who hated the idea of having to get up and speak in front of anyone. Look at you now, just as confident as you want to be.

I know growing up it was hard. So many people told you what you couldn't do and doubted your ability to succeed. That chip you carry around on your shoulder has served as quite the motivational tool, hasn't it?

I also love that you still take the time out to talk to the Lord and thank him, because you understand where your blessings come from.

You keep on pressing forward, okay? Don't let anything stop you, because there will be more obstacles that come your way now more than ever, now that you have tasted a little bit of the success you crave. Don't let the haters get to you.

A lot of people are counting on you. Whether you know it or not, people look up to you and are watching your every move.

Stay focused! You can accomplish anything you set your mind to. You are destined for greatness.

Love,
Determination

I fell in love with this thing,
before I even knew what love was.

Since I didn't know how to say it,
I wrote a letter . . .

You know that feeling you get when your song comes on the radio? It doesn't matter how many times you hear it: the jam is the jam.

They say there's a song for every situation you're going through. Whether you're happy, sad, depressed, heartbroken, or excited, a song can always express how you feel. Or just the opposite, music has a way of helping you tap into your emotions or reveal an insight about something inside you that you didn't even know was there to begin with.

There is nothing like that hot beat, killer verse, or five-part harmony.

What would we do without music? What a magnificent art form.

I'm writing this letter to you, Music, because I want you to know how much you have done for me.

You helped me set the mood; you even got me out of tough situations after I messed up with that special someone.

I can't thank you enough. You are in my heart, mind, and soul. You allow me to move to the beat of my own drum, because from the moment I heard you, we became one.

Thanks again.

Love,
Melody

*This person really made me the man who I am,
but I could never quite say what I wanted to say.*

So I wrote a letter instead . . .

Hey Dad,

I'm all grown up now, but yet I still can't quite find the words to say what I've wanted to say all these years. You know, as a kid, I always wondered if I made you proud. It's funny, because even now that I'm an adult, I still wonder the same thing.

When I was a kid, you were hard on me. I guess you felt you needed to be because I was the boy, and that's what fathers do to their only sons. As an adult, now I'm hard on myself because I know I still have work to do.

As a kid, I didn't want to be like you. I wanted to be better than you. It's funny, because as an adult, in my own way, I hope to be just like you.

I've never seen you call in sick or just take a day off. As a kid, I couldn't understand it. As an adult, I appreciate it and marvel at it.

You kept a roof over my head, and for as long as I can remember, I've always had the best of everything.

Yeah, at times it was hard to ask you for anything, but I can't really recall a time when I asked you for something and you said "no."

How cool is that?

As a kid, I didn't really agree with everything you did. I know you feel I'm closer to Mom, but as an adult, I value our relationship just the same.

I am one of the lucky ones, because I had my father with me every step of the way. For that, I thank you.

Love,
Your Son

*Have you ever been on an airplane and realized
you were the only person paying attention?*

It's absolutely frustrating.

*I had to pull out a pen and a notepad
just to keep myself from getting up and saying
what the employees wouldn't say . . .*

Thank you very much for your business. Heaven knows, I would be unemployed without it. I do love what I do because sometimes I only work a few days a week. You can't beat that with a bat! However, I have to be perfectly honest. In this line of work, I deal with adults for the most part, but you would never know it from the way they act.

I do my very best to give clear, concise instructions to keep everyone safe and sound. I even let my passengers know information before they need to know it.

I suppose I'm not quite as honest as I could be with the passengers because I want to keep my good job. I know they do hear me when I speak, because I have the loudspeaker at my disposal. So, if you hear me so well Mr. and Ms. Passenger, why do you still stand up after I say all passengers must be seated with seats upright and tray tables secured before takeoff? Would it be too much to ask you just to wait a few minutes until we are airborne?

In addition, when I shut the cabin door, you know what's going to come next, so why do you torture me? Put those darn electronic devices away and don't play games with me. Please remove your headphones. That makes me nervous.

By the way, this plane is not Mango's in Miami, the Velvet Room in Atlanta, or the Enclave in Chicago. Those are incredible, second-to-none night spots, so stop trying to order drinks like you're there already. If you are in dire need of something besides a beer, jack and Coke, or wine, you are in the wrong place.

Okay, now I can breathe.

By the way, first-class cabin, I'm happy for you. Congratulations on whatever has afforded you the opportunity to sit in the front. Some of you should lighten up though. The seat doesn't make you first-class: you should be first-class before and after you sit down.

Now, I'd like for you all to sit back, relax, and enjoy your flight, your day, or wherever else destiny may take you.

Sincerely,
Fly Right

All the hitting, throwing,
and berating were becoming a little too much to handle,

so all I could do was write this letter . . .

What did I do? Why are you hurting me? When you do this, we both suffer. You do know that don't you? Did you really just attempt to throw me completely across the room?

You damn near broke my entire face. Sweetheart, I can barely see now. I know you're upset, but what happened to dealing with things sensibly?

I know it seems bad, but I'm sure it'll get better. What would it matter if I'm gone once everything does get better? All that beating would have been done in vain.

Listen, I deal with all of your moods. When you're happy, I'm there for your laughter. When you're sad, I feel the tears, and when you're angry . . . look out!

When do I get a break or a little appreciation, maybe a protective shield, cover, or jacket?

You hold me like nobody else, so please, no more abuse, and can you please quit dropping me?

Yours,
Repaired Cell Phone

*Ladies, there's something I really wanted to
get off my chest.*

*I'm sure this issue applies
to more guys than just me.*

*Regardless, I need to say something because
it's something I've had to deal with time and time again.*

I hope writing this down helps.

At least I feel a little better already . . .

I see you. I just saw that look. If I were walking with a black woman, would I have gotten your attention? Despite popular belief, this woman holding my hand and feeling the stares pierce her has looked out for and loved me like you may or may not have.

I have never left home. I have never forgotten where I came from either. My mom and two sisters are beautiful black women, and I love them dearly in addition to my aunts, grandmothers, and everyone else in my life. I remember where I came from and where they came from, and I will never forget what it all entails.

If you're so upset, the next time you see someone like me, I invite you to come across the aisle, to the front of the line, or to wherever we are and simply ask me why. Maybe the answer won't soothe your soul, but it will simply answer your question, and you can choose how you want to feel afterward. You might give a regular brother with potential a chance next time, who knows?

Maybe you won't, or maybe you're upset for the sister who might actually want me. This person next to me was next to me when I had nothing. She helps me out, and on more than one occasion, she has given me her last something if I needed it. I am not lost. I am fully aware of the relationship I am in and why I am in it.

I love and respect black women. That will grow through the end of time. no matter who I end up with. Love me the same and don't let that love change once you see me walking by myself again.

I hope you love yourself and/or your significant other as much as you want the "right" love for me.

Truly,
Good Brother

*It was driving me crazy to see people
being more bold on the Internet than they
would ever be in person.*

*I thought I might be too harsh if I picked
up the phone, so I wrote a letter . . .*

You think you're slick, don't you.

We are cool, and yes, we talk fairly often, but we're nothing too serious.

How did you get the courage to leave me that kind of comment? And of all things, you left it on Myspace.

Part of me thinks it's funny because you knew I was going to be on a plane the last time we spoke. When I left, there was nothing online. But when I got off the plane, I opened my laptop while waiting for my connecting flight, only to see a comment that would suggest something with you other than friendship. You are something else.

I suppose now you think I'll have to answer to someone about this, which may be true, but realize I can take two steps back. Why would you get so bold now? We are not that close.

Maybe next time you feel that brave you'll pick up the phone, but you'll be satisfied to know that regardless it won't be me on the other end. Next time think of a better idea.

I've heard of people being silly like this, but I didn't think I knew any of those people. It's cool. Just so you know, that is hardly game and even less mature. Have a good one and I'll "see" you around, no writing necessary.

Sincerely,
Dot Com Backslash

*Have you ever felt like you were down
to your last straw?*

*It's tough to strive when it feels like
everything is weighing you down.*

*I had that feeling at the most random
moment, so I took the time to
write this letter . . .*

As I sit here in one of my favorite fast food restaurants, nothing seems quite right. Nothing seems like where it's supposed to be.

At the same time, it feels like I am exactly where I'm supposed to be. It's tough though.

As I type one letter after another, I feel a tear forming in my right eye. I can hold it back though. I'm stronger than that.

Does crying mean I'm not strong? I feel like I'm reaching my breaking point and I need something or someone to hold me up and hold the tears back.

One moment please, my phone is ringing. It's my sister! I was just asking for someone or something! She didn't even know what she had just done for me, but she did it. As she asked me how I was doing, I told her I was fine and I needed her call more than she knew. She said she was glad. As she said that, tears streamed down my face as though my eyelids had opened the gates.

I fought through the tears, and the stress in my voice quickly turned into laughter.

Life is great and I am blessed. I almost lost it.

Has anyone ever called you or spoke to you when you needed it the most? The fact that your prayer is answered is almost as moving as the call or message.

Okay, I'm pulling myself together now. Trouble doesn't last forever, and if you put your mind, your heart, and your effort into your dream or your task it will come through. Never lose faith.

We all reach that point where we think we're lost, but someone is always there to see us through. Pick up the phone and tell someone how great he or she is. I guarantee that person will appreciate it.

So now what? I dust myself off, grab some tissues from the table, and push forward. I can and will do this.

Sincerely,
Keep Your Head Up

*Have you ever met someone who came on stronger
than Brut aftershave?*

*When it's not the right person,
it feels so wrong.*

We have all had that experience.

*What better way to express it
than through a letter . . .*

Please. Please. Please! Slow down. I like you too.

Damn, where did you come from? Thanks for the early birthday, late Christmas, and Sweetest Day gift. I know I said we should hang out sometime, but I didn't know you meant right now.

Did you just say what I think you said? No, we can wait to meet each other's parents, because you may be crazy tomorrow or even establish a new record and be crazy before I do anything wrong or too much right.

I'm bored already. Do you realize you told me everything about you in our first few conversations? Do you even know my last name? At first, I thought I was being too hard on you or setting my expectations too high, but that's not the case. They are right where they're supposed to be.

I thought you'd make me work a little bit harder, but that's not the case at all. Quite honestly, it doesn't seem fair. I'm the one scratching my head thinking to myself, "am I this good"? At times like this, that is a harder question than it seems to be.

How about this: can you relax just a bit before it's too

late? You are nice and I do like you, but you need to take two steps back; otherwise, there is no way this can work out. I don't know if this is your normal approach, but scale it back a little bit. Give me a reason to call back and think of you when you aren't around.

Okay, that's a lot better. At least I won't go completely nuts today.

Truthfully,
Too Much Too Soon

Have you ever been dressed to go out
and knew you were going to own the place?

I've had a few of those nights.

What better way to express it than in a letter . . .

Tonight is the night! I walked out of the house and felt like the world was at my fingertips. Maybe it was the subtle yet sexy haircut. Maybe it was the sophisticated cocktail dress accompanied by the cutest shoes that didn't even hurt my feet, which made for better walking and a sassier demeanor. (Ladies, we all know how it can be walking in those corn busters. They seem like a good idea at first, or shall I say those first few minutes.)

When I walked in, I swear the club was playing my theme music, "Miss Independent" by Ne-Yo. The crowd parted as if Moses were my escort for the evening. I had a great time all night, and I paid for each and every one of my drinks. I even bought a drink for a good-looking gentleman who acted as such. I had decent conversations; I danced with my girlfriends and waved at those looking just to look. It was all fun.

I got plenty of attention and that was not even the plan. It felt like I was in the zone. People looked at me as if I were one of the beautiful people. They didn't stare at me because I had my butt hanging out or plenty of cleavage present. I think they paid more attention because it was clear I paid attention to myself. I am only 5'4", but I walked as if I were six feet tall. I walked like I was someone and carried myself the same way.

I had the best time, and I think I need to have more

days and nights like this one. I felt empowered on my own terms. This is how it should be. I feel great and want to keep feeling like this. The best part is I now realize I am the one in control of that feeling.

Thank you, and I'll see you next time I'm out.

Truly,
Real Woman

Going out doesn't have to be about finding a mate.
It is about enjoying yourself,
and seeing others do the same.

This letter is about one of those nights...

Tonight was a great night. It was one of the best.

All right, I have to be honest. It was another regular night for me. Whether you are a male or female, I'm sure you've had that feeling that screamed, "I love being me!" Yes, that's the feeling we unknowingly crave sometimes.

I was dressed and ready to go at a reasonable hour and arrived at this venue earlier than most, but I am always all right with that. I am not anxious, I just like to arrive and chill and enjoy the atmosphere before all of the controlled chaos begins.

I dressed well, and I smiled all night. Sometimes people think I'm up to something because I smile for no reason at all. Back in the day, women were the only ones to walk around as if they owned the place, but not anymore. My walk says I am a force to be reckoned with, my gestures suggest confidence, not arrogance, and my subtle approach says prepare yourself, whoever you are, because this is going to be one hell of an experience.

I heard what I hear so often: it feels like I've known you forever. It has been a gift and a curse at times. I love to put smiles on faces. Maybe it is a control issue, but put a smile on someone's face, and see how it makes you feel. You may very well get addicted like me.

I walked by a group of friends and offered to take a picture of them as they decided who was going to have to sit out on this one. "No need to worry, I got it," I said. It was a nice gesture, and I left quietly as I waved and responded to their thank you with "you're welcome" and nothing more.

It was even better when someone walked up and stood next to me to order a drink. I introduced myself and initiated a short conversation. When it was time to pay, I took care of it. That was not the powerful part. The powerful part was saying "have a good evening" and walking away without hesitation. That action was noted and remembered.

The night was mine once again, and it felt like it was supposed to feel. I went home alone, happy and with the dignity I came in with.

How about you?

Sincerely,
Distinguished

*I started wondering whether
I was really a "good man."*

*Instead of talking to someone about it,
I decided to write a letter . . .*

Dear Me,

What does it really mean to be a "good man?" Am I a good man because I work hard and have a job? Am I a good man because I believe in God and say my prayers at night? Am I a good man because I don't live at home with my mother and I have my own home? Am I a good man because I still believe in opening doors for women, pulling out chairs, and sending flowers and candy?

Do any of these things make me a good man? I don't know, because if I'm being honest with you, I've lied to women. I've made women feel a certain way about me, all the while knowing I had no intentions of feeling the same about them. As the saying goes, I am guilty of "telling women what they want to hear" for my own personal gain and agenda. I have wined and dined women with no intention of being in a relationship—for no other reason than to say I had her, or to prove to myself I could get her if I set my mind to it.

Don't get me wrong, I don't disrespect any women. When a woman is with me, she will feel like she is the only woman in the room. I'm very smooth (or at least I like to think so), but does that make me a good man?

I will always answer my phone when a woman calls, and if I am busy, I will be sure to return her call. Does that make me a good man?

Am I a good man because I will rub your feet after a long day? Or run your bath water and give you a massage without you having to ask for it?

Ladies, what does a "good man" mean to you? Is the good man the one who doesn't get caught, or is the good man the one who convinces you he is good?

I don't know why I started to question whether I am really a good man. I feel like I am because I know I mean well.

I guess I wrote this letter to you because I hear so many women say they want a "good man," but I wonder whether they really know the definition for that term, because I don't.

Sincerely,
Casanova

Have you ever been stressed out
by something you had no control over?
I have,

so I decided to express it in this letter . . .

Hey there,

It's me again. I know you're probably tired of hearing from me, but no matter how hard you try, I'm going to always be here. Even until the day you die, I will be a part of your life now that you are an adult.

I know you look back on it now and you really enjoyed being a kid. You didn't have to worry about me back then, because someone else took care of me for you.

Man, you really do have a great support system, because sometimes they still help you take care of me, don't they? Yeah, I bet you thought I didn't know, but I remember that month when you were a little short and you asked your mom and dad for a favor. You almost scared me one time, because you came pretty darn close to paying me off, but I knew you couldn't stay away too long.

As I said before, I am going to always be a part of your life now. You can't enjoy some of the simple pleasures in life without going through me first. I mean stuff like having a roof over your head, lights to turn on and off, or that all-important telephone you love so much. Oh, let's not forget that television you are glued to some days.

No one single thing will have more of an impact on your life than me, and now that you've finished college, you and I have become extremely close. Don't worry though, you're not alone. I am friends with everyone who owns something or who is responsible for keeping something going in America. Essentially that's life, so welcome to it. I'm certain I will hear from you again next month. Until then, take care . . .

Sincerely,
Paying Bills

PS: Sorry about that time I had to cut you off for a while. You took too long to come and see me.

Have you ever met someone,
and from the moment you laid eyes
on that person, you knew you wanted
to find out more about him or her?

I have, so I decided to write a letter about it . . .

Let me tell you about last night. I was standing in line, about to attend one of the hottest parties of the year—or at least that's what I was told it would be.

While waiting to get in, I noticed this woman who had a style and a look like I've never seen. She walked with such a confidence that other women in line couldn't help but make comments. We were standing near each other, but for some reason I thought it would be corny to try and talk to her while standing in line. I know other guys do that, and as I looked around there was a lot of that going on, but that's just not me. So I told myself, I would see her inside, so exercise some patience and wait for the right time to make my move.

I was told this would be one of the hottest parties of the year, but I had no idea what was in store. When I walked in, the crowd was huge, and I thought to myself, there is no way I'm going to find this woman again. Now I was upset I didn't speak when I had the chance. They say to take advantage of an opportunity when it presents itself, because you never know if it will come around again.

I decided to still make the most of my night. It was a very good night, and let me say I had it all working for me: I looked good and smelled good, and my swagger was on full display. Every woman I approached seemed interested, and several women approached me expressing their interest. Out of all this attention I received, no one was quite as intriguing as the woman I had seen in line. As I worked my way around that night dancing, engaging in conversation, and just having an overall good time, I still hoped I would run into my mystery woman.

The night continued to wind down, and I gave up on the idea of running into her. The crowd was so large it was like trying to find a needle in a haystack.

As I headed toward the door, I just so happened to look to my left. There she was! I'd waited all night to cross paths with her, and there she was again. So I casually walked over and attempted to get her to notice me, but she wasn't paying any attention to me. She was standing there with one of her girlfriends, and her girlfriend was actually the one who helped me out. Her friend tapped her on her arm, as if to say "girl, look at him." It is always a good thing to get the girlfriend's "stamp of approval." As she finally looked at me, we smiled at one another and exchanged pleasantries. After a few moments, I stepped up and gave her my information and asked her to call me sometime. She replied, "I wouldn't be having this conversation with you if I wasn't going to call you." We smiled again, and I thought to myself, beautiful and sassy—what a combination.

Just when I was about to give up and leave for the night, the cards turned in my favor and I was able to make my presence known to her. Sure, I've met a lot of women in my time, but there is something special about this one, and I can't quite put my finger on it. So I guess we will see how it goes . . .

Thanks,
Guy from the Club

This needed to be said,
but who would admit to it?

So I wrote a letter
to get it out instead . . .

Hey there,

I just wanted to let you know I think about you all the time. I know I'm not the only one, because a lot of my friends talk about you all the time too. It's so funny how they try and make it seem as if men are the only ones who think about you all the time, but I know some women who value you just as much as I do.

How did you become so powerful? Did you know you are a big reason why some relationships don't last? I'm sure you knew. If I'm being honest, you have affected some of my relationships. I've stopped dating people because of you, and I've even cheated on a few people because I was looking for or wanting a better version of you.

Trust me, I'm not complaining about you, because hey, I love you very much. When I got my first chance to meet you, I knew I would never be the same again. As a matter of fact, I remember the first time we met like it was yesterday. I think after that day I lost my damn mind, and I wondered why it took me so long to meet you in the first place. I mean, everybody else around seemed to know you already, and some knew you quite well at an early age. No, I'm not going to say any names, I'm sure you know who they are.

I heard you were good, but wow—I didn't know you were that good. I mean think about it, I can turn on my television and see you every day if I want. Companies even use you on a daily basis to help sell their products. You sure are powerful; I think you have more power than the President of the United States. Hell, even a few of them have loved you a little too much. ☒

I know you mean well and you've always wanted people to be safe and smart about dealing with you. I guess without you I wouldn't be here writing this letter.

I hope this letter finds you well, and by the time you read this we will have probably crossed paths again.

So be good, and I mean that in every sense of the word.

Yours Truly,
Sex

*Have you ever felt as
if you may have met the perfect person for you?*

Who are they?

Where are they?

Who is heaven's choice for you?

One day I woke up, and for some reason I felt today would be different from any other I had awaken to before.

That day was so weird, so strange, so out of the ordinary, I couldn't really explain it.

I was in the right place at the wrong time. Let me say that again—I was in the right place at the wrong time. Let me explain . . .

The first time I saw her, I tried to get her attention, but I was too late. The first time I saw her, I lost all concept of where I was at the time.

She had no idea about me. She had no idea that in a brief instant she would change my life forever.

She was the greatest distraction, the greatest stumbling block, and the greatest challenge. The crazy thing about that is I never even said "hello."

So that's it, right? She was there one moment and gone the next. There was no way for me to find out who she was.

She had returned to her life, not knowing I even existed. I couldn't function the rest of that unordinary day because I felt like I was one step too slow, a day late, and a dollar short.

Before I got upset with myself, before I let anger take over my excitement, I asked, how this could be?

Can God reveal heaven's choice for me?

I was so tired of the everyday routine: meet a woman and spend a little time with her, only to lose interest or to find out she wasn't what she said she was after all.

So I played the game with the best of them: I became the king of breaking hearts and taking names.

Telling myself living the life of a bachelor, of a playboy, of a pimp, and of Romeo is cool.

I thought I was calling the shots and in control. Who was I kidding? My heart yearned for something more. I started to lose faith in truly knowing what love is, what being happy with a woman is all about.

Now I know no one is perfect, but I did believe there was a perfect fit for me. They say patience is a virtue, but I ran out of patience for heartache, confusion, and pain. Does God in heaven have a choice for me? Had I done too much to get my prayers answered? Had I not done enough? Had I told too many lies and half-truths to gain the divine favor of a good woman? I could understand if that was the case.

So just like any other day, I awoke to begin my everyday life. I got out of bed, did my daily routine, picked something to wear, got dressed, and went off to work.

Upon arriving at work, I was told I was going to be sitting in on the new hire training since my position was about to change.

When I arrived, I couldn't believe my eyes. The woman who I thought I would never see again—the one I let get away—was right in front of me! Was this a joke? Was this a cruel prank? Was I dreaming? If I walk up and pinch her to see if she's real, will she think I'm crazy?

I wouldn't make the same mistake twice. I knew what I had to do. I knew it was time to make my move.

What are the chances this beautiful woman, who I saw for a brief moment in time, would resurface in such a close way? Who knew I would have the chance for me to see her every day if I wanted?

So I set out to show her that I was the one for her, and that she and I should become one. After a lot of sweat and tears, she agreed.

God works in mysterious ways. He always has the answer. He will show up when you need Him.

Sincerely,
Heaven's Choice for Me

Have you ever messed up,
and when you tried to
go back and correct your mistakes, it was too late?

This letter will
take you there . . .

So is this your way of telling me to give up? I mean Saturday, Sunday, and now Monday have passed, and I know you got all of my messages and calls.

Is it really so bad that you can't talk to me? Is it really so bad that you feel you have to continue to run from me? Because you know that's what you are doing and what you did even when we were talking.

What else do you want me to say? I've owned up to my mistakes and apologized. What more can I do?

You can't tell me things are so serious with this guy you're "seeing" that you're going to shut me out.

Come on woman, is that how it is? Life is about choices, and you have a choice here . . .

So if it's really like that, then I'll fall back. Just know I was serious about my intent. I hope you are getting all that you want—I truly do.

Love,
One More Chance

*Have you ever had one of those arguments
where everything came out wrong?*

*You both were actually agreeing,
but nothing came out right,
and you needed to make amends?*

I did, and this was the letter I wrote . . .

As I sit here, by myself, in little old Tulsa, I think . . . and think . . . and think . . .

After our conversation tonight, I want you to know that from the bottom of my heart, I can't even begin to describe how I feel about you . . . love isn't even the right word.

Maybe I'm tripping, but love is something that brings two people together. So what is it that makes people stay together for a lifetime?

Whatever that might be is what I am feeling . . . I love you so much it hurts. At times I tell myself, I love her too much, what's next?

Baby, if it were practical, I want you to know that I am truly in a time in my life where I would give myself away to you . . . I would marry you tomorrow . . . promise . . .

For us to get through these tough times we need to realize our day will come . . . we just need to clear the speed bumps in our path (one more year of school!) and we will begin the most beautiful, strong, and loving family in the world . . .

We can do this . . . TOGETHER . . .

I adore you.

Sincerely,
Trying Harder

If you've never thanked your big sister,
let her know how great she is and
how much you appreciate her.

I don't do this often enough,
so I wanted to send this letter . . .

Hey dude! I hope you're well. I know people see us hanging out and besides thinking we are absolutely beautiful, they wonder why are we laughing or how we get along so well. First off, they should know that isn't always the case, but we do the best we can.

You keep it real for me even when I don't want to hear it. You know, I still remember you taking me places because you were the oldest. As I think back, I never remember you making me feel bad when you had to take me someplace. You always made sure I was fed and that I had a good time. You always made sure your friends looked after me as if I were their little brother.

Funny enough, you still do the same thing. You do for others before you do for yourself sometimes, which drives me crazy. It makes you a lot like Mom, doesn't it? You're both incredible, beautiful people. Even though you're the big sister, you always respect me and make me feel special. I find myself thinking of ways to repay you, even though the time and love you put in cannot be matched.

I just want you to know that I know. You are the best, and as I get older, I appreciate every day just as much as the next. You have made bad days good and good days better.

Thank you for being you and the type of sister every sibling wishes for.

Love,
Little Brother

Have you ever had one of those
moments when you said I love you,
and there was silence on the other end
or a semi-awkward smile?

There's a reason why that happens, so
I wrote this letter . . .

Sweetheart,

First and foremost, I want to thank you for everything you do for me. I truly appreciate it so much.

I love everything you've done for me, from the way you have completely changed my life to the little everyday things you say and do that help brighten my day.

I absolutely love the things you send me in the mail and the trips you have made to come see me.

You mean everything to me. It's hard to put the way you have touched my life and make me feel in words.

I know it is a little harder for me to express myself but, baby, I can't hold my true feelings in any longer.

Baby, I LOVE YOU from the bottom of my heart.

The way you push my buttons on the inside is incredible. I can't wait to see what our future holds. I wanted to wait and tell you while I was holding you close to me, but Baby, after this last weekend, I couldn't hold back my feelings any longer.

You are amazing.

Truly,
The Man of Your Dreams

Even though I don't always tell you,
there's something I have to confess....

There are little things that happen every once and awhile that let me know the love I have for you is genuine and real.

Saying goodbye to you is one of the hardest things for me to do.

I think I break down every time because it feels like I am watching the best thing that has ever happened to me turn and walk away.

Even when you are out of sight, you are permanently in my mind.

Saying that "you complete me" takes away from our equation.

I would say you are the extra in my life.

You make me want to be better for you and our future.

Your absence makes me really cherish each and every moment we have together.

I can't wait for the day when we will be able to be together forever.

I adore you.

Truly,
Long Distance

You know, sometimes someone sends you something and you keep it with you all the time so you never forget it.

I keep this letter in my wallet 24/7 . . .

I love this man who makes my life complete and fulfilling.

He makes every sunrise brighter and every sunset more beautiful.

In his eyes I see my future. I see the completion of one part of my life and the beginning of another part of my life.

When I think about him, my heart smiles and frowns at the same time. It smiles for the future we have, but it frowns at the obstacles we face before we will get to that future.

In the end, he will he will always be my other half, and the key holder to my everlasting love.

I wish I had the ability to tell him how much I love him every second of the day, but I can't because I would run out of breath.

I want him to know I cherish him and admire everything about him.

You are my life, my love, and my inspiration.

Truly,
Your True Love

*There are moments that a father and son
experience that are groundbreaking.*

*These moments catapult their
relationship to a new place.*

*I wanted to describe that place,
so I wrote a letter . . .*

In truth, for most of my life, you seemed untouchable, Dad. I respected you because you helped create the family. You went to work every day, even though it wasn't your typical dream job. It was a dream job in a sense, because it made dreams come true. What you worked so hard for helped make my dreams come true.

You never asked for too much in return either. You wanted hard work and appreciation. All that being said, I was intimidated by you. I know that sounds crazy, but it is true. You are respected by so many; you've rubbed elbows with the best of them, including President Barack Obama—literally!

However, one road trip took everything to a different place.

It did not—I repeat—it did not start out well. My heart fell to my stomach when I realized the air conditioning in the car wasn't working and we were headed to Southwest Texas. The more unnerving part was that I had to tell you. Great start!

We did finally hit the road. We had decent weather throughout, and although we threatened to roll into Southwest Texas in only our boxers and tank tops, we didn't have to. For the first time in my life, I knew what it was like to laugh so hard you cry with a person who loves you more than you know.

It took me back to all our hard talks I took so personally. Those were "I love you" talks. It also took me back to getting whipped. And while you and mom claim it hurt you more than it hurt me, that may be the only thing I can emphatically disagree with. We talked, we joked, we listened to music, and we sat in total silence. It was a new beginning for me and the man whose name I carry.

We arrived in town and I was safe, sound, and moved in with all of your help. You never made me feel like I owed you anything, although I owed you everything.

I took you to the airport a few days later, and as you walked away, I felt like my dad and my best friend were both leaving at the same time. No pictures were taken and no journals were signed, but everything was where it was supposed to be.

This was the best trip of my life and it didn't involve beaches or Mai Tais. This is exactly what we needed.

Love,
Road Trip

Have you ever had a feeling something might
be going on, but you just couldn't put
your finger on it?

I had one of those feelings,
but instead of blowing up,
I thought I'd just write this letter...

I saw the text . . . decided to wait awhile so you wouldn't know I'd peeked.

I saw the name, the consistent conversation, and I wondered how long this had been going on . . . for weeks?

But you played the game and thought I didn't know. You thought you were being discreet.

But silence isn't always consent—
You see, sometimes it can be altered deceit.

Now when my phone rings, don't look surprised when I giggle and press delete.

You just tend to your phone and your conversation . . . what you sow . . . that will you reap.

Hey, don't worry your brain trying to figure it out with multiple outrageous guesses, just blame it on technology today . . . dang those darn text messages.

Sincerely,
Inbox

Fellas, have you ever heard that infamous phrase,
"I've never done this or that before?"

Well, I have.

Instead of bursting out into laughter,
.   I wrote this letter . . .

Well, well, well. We meet again.

Guys, we get such a hard time about this kind of stuff. We just remain silent, but we are sometimes forced to reply with "me either." Yeah, right? And this isn't exactly what you think it is. It falls under all kinds of categories. This first kiss, giving your number out, freaky deaky dancing, and the big you-know-what! Right! I hear you, and sweetheart, I am not judging you. I'm not giving you that look—just don't give me that naive look when you're treated how you act.

I think it's even funnier when that's said about a bodily function. You know what I mean when one slips through the cracks. Dun Dun Dunnnn. Yeah, we know you have before, even if you tried to leave the room. It followed that cute little tush of yours right back in. It's okay, we all do it. I am not here to judge you.

I know that as an adult, I doubt all of your firsts have come with me, from the kiss to the couch to everything under the sun, and that's okay.

Thank you for painting the picture of holiness, but in all reality, those things are what make you the person you are and the people we are together. Not to mention they'll make one heck of a joke 20 years from now.

It's crazy writing a letter, because usually I never do this.

Sincerely,
First Time

Sometimes we need a pep talk,
but no one is there to give it to us.

What better person than the person directly involved?

I wrote this letter to you hopefully to cheer you up! I know lately your heart has been so heavy with so many things. I know there are times when you feel so overwhelmed and it seems like you just can't get on solid ground.

I've been sitting back just observing the woman you are—the woman you've become with every trial and tribulation you've faced. Each one has chiseled you into the beautiful sculpture you are today. You know that's how sculptures start out, right—as big slabs of marble— and then the sculptor comes along with a hammer and a chisel and he starts going to work. He starts banging and carving away at the unwanted pieces of marble, and with each piece that falls, more beauty evolves.

Tab, that perfectly describes you. Your life has been a series of events since you were a little girl—your mother's drug addiction and all the pain it caused, losing your mother to her addiction, being torn away from your brother and sister, becoming a young mother and then a young wife, going through a divorce, suffering through a series of bad relationships, losing close relatives to violence, losing jobs, raising two children as a single mother, and the list continues . . .

But you have not allowed adversity to bring you down. Actually you've done just the opposite—you've used it as fuel to make you fight harder and be stronger. You've found purpose in it—you've strengthened your relationship with God because of it. You took all the things intended to take you out and used them take you higher!

I know the struggle has been rough for you, and I know some days you just want to throw in the white towel. You want to throw your hands up and say "I quit—I can't do this anymore." But I applaud you for not doing that. Instead, you say "Lord, I'm tired and I'm laying my burdens down for you to handle—for your Word says it's not my battle, it's the Lord's." I see you cry sometimes when you're sitting down trying to figure out how you're going to pay all the bills, buy food, have gas, and still be able to make it through the week. I've marveled at how you juggle all your bills and still manage to step out of the house looking like a million bucks.

I sometimes even envy you. I've seen you in a room with other women who've spent all kinds of money on their hair, their nails, and their clothes and accessories, and then I see you and you're flawless. You're on their level if not higher, and I say to myself, "how does she do it?" Then you told me, "I did my own hair and makeup, I also do my own manicures and pedicures, and I'm a helluva bargain shopper." All I can say is "you did that!"

I'm also writing you this letter because I know there are still some things you beat yourself up about. You have unfinished business, things you've started such as school and your career that you've put on hold. I want to tell you the time has come for you to step up and start to make things happen.

I see your struggles with these dead-end jobs, I see your frustrations as you try to make ends meet, and I see your dreams deferred.

I know all of the things you wish you had, and I hear you when you say if I had the money to do this I'd . . .

Tab, I love you. So I have to tell you to stop

procrastinating and put a plan into action. Yes, you're a fantastic mom, you're a provider and a friend and so many other great things—but you have to start taking care of yourself as well. Once you start to do that, a lot of the frustrations you have will begin to disappear.

Now don't get me wrong, I'm not telling you that you won't still have problems—we all will always have to deal with conflict—but if you want a better life, then you have to make a better life for yourself and for your children.

Make the time for you, Tab, and make the most out of it. Remember to keep God first in all you do, and always remember that tough times don't last but tough people do!

Stay blessed.

Love,
Your Inner Self

I don't always open up,
but you are all over and inside of me.
I do thank the heavens for you.

Hopefully, you'll understand once you read this letter . . .

Dear Love,

I know I play a big responsibility in our failures. My pride allows me to say I don't need you, and my machismo forces me to believe I am weak if I need you. Truth is, I do need you, I yearn for you, and I would die to have you. I need you more than you will ever know. Unfortunately, if I allowed you to know this, I would make myself vulnerable, naked at your feet, unable to hide any of my inner insecurities. My ego tells you that you should be happy to be with me, but deep down inside, I thank God for giving me such a wonderful blessing. I demand your every second, your undivided attention because that is what I am willing to give you. Sadly, I rarely display it. I hear your moans of discontent and dissatisfaction, yet I can only admit to them in the privacy of thought. I fear that if I admitted my wrongs, you would leave.

My passion for you recklessly drives my life's motivations. I want—no, I must have you be proud of me. I accuse you of not understanding me but offer very little to help you achieve the insight. You only want my love, never knowing that is all I have for you. I worship the ground you walk on. It saddens me to see your pain. You would never know I drown from the tears that pour within my heart from remorse. I am cursed to not understand the significance of fidelity and a reluctance to face the unknowing. I can admit I cheat on you often with my soul's temptation, placing everything I don't need in front of my lifeline. I consistently use your name in vain, diminishing your unequivocal value with every word I whisper. I see so many abandon your presence, afraid of what they have never known. I too have given up on you with a shaky confidence and silent sadness. You are attached to my soul and intertwined with my destiny, so I recognize our romance is never over. My lips want to caress your ear with the words "I will never leave." I concede my greatest fear is one day you will not be by my side. You are a constant pillar of my life. I escape in the warmth of your bosom. I feel guarded, cloaked in an impenetrable armor of admiration. I want to give you the world; however, I realize you don't need it to feel the satisfaction of joy. Your touch is my heavenly inspiration, although I pretend your affection annoys me. Intimidation runs through my veins due to my inability to accept that I am worthy of you. Maybe your absence in my youth is the reason I find it hard to believe I deserve you. I'm sick of running from what is right and embracing what is wrong. I stand before you willing to give you all that I am and all that I will be. Complete my soul, fulfill my life, give me your love, and conquer my heart.

Sincerely,
Man

*I knew someone who was playing
hard to get.*

*I got tired of playing her game,
so I decided to write a letter . . .*

I know you like me, so why are you acting like you don't? It was cute at first, but come on, who are you trying to fool?

When I see you out and about, you try to act like I'm not there, but you're quick to call me the next day and tell me every single detail about every woman you saw talking to me. Now what's that all about?

Yeah, we are good friends and we get along really well, but remember that time we almost kissed? It was like one of those moments you see in the movies. They say you should be friends with someone first anyway, right? So I think that base is covered.

I know you like me, so why are you acting like you don't? Do you think if we cross that line, we won't be able to go back?

You remember when I was out of town for a while on business and I came back? You were upset when you found out I was home and your place wasn't the first or second stop I made? Why is that?

It's so funny how every time I ask you to hook me up with one your girlfriends, they quickly turn from your best friends to your worst enemies.

How come every woman I tell you about "isn't good enough for me" and you've always got something negative to say, but when I drop hints at you about you and me, all of a sudden you draw a blank?

It's time to throw all our cards on the table and say how we really feel about each other, because if you don't like me you sure have a funny way of showing that you don't.

Maybe I'll slide you a note one day that says, "Do you like me? Circle yes or no." Maybe then you will reveal your secret. Because I know you like me, even though you try to act like you don't.

Love,
I Don't Want to be "Just Friends" Anymore

So if women are from Venus
and men are from Mars,
then I must be from somewhere else altogether.

I wrote about it in this letter . . .

So let me just keep it real. What's the big deal with all this Love stuff anyway? I mean people act like it's a law that says you have to fall in love—like you're missing out on something so big if you don't.

Well, I don't know if I buy into all that. Why can't I just have fun, do my thing, and enjoy life without having to hear about the "joys of love"?

When I look around, all I see are reasons why I shouldn't fall in love. And marriage—HA! Yeah, right. What is the statistic—like over 50% of all marriages in the U.S. end in divorce these days? Why would I want to look forward to that? In my dating experience, I've had married women offer themselves to me. I've had women who claimed to be so "in love" and in relationships who still wanted to date me on the side. Is that what it means to be in love? If so, then I don't want it.

How is someone supposed to fight all the temptation out there anyway? Women outnumber men by the thousands, and men come on so strong that women can't fight that hard.

Think about it, every time you ask someone "how's married life treating you?", the response always includes "it's hard." Why does it have to be so hard? I had to work hard in school to succeed, and I work hard on my job, but why do I have to work hard to stay happy in a relationship? Is that a job I'm really trying to apply for? I don't think so.

Love sounds too much like stress to me. Maybe someone will write me back with a different perspective, but as for now, Love can take a backseat.

Sincerely,
Skeptical One

*We often have a special message solely
for one special person.*

This is that message.

*Maybe you should write your own
special message too.*

He used to be here . . .

I'm writing this letter . . . please place it in your pocket;
if you should see him pass it along.

Don't be so inquisitive about what the letter entails;
I'll read it aloud so you will know . . .

But before I do please promise me that its contents
you will hide; for what I'm sharing is confidential, and in
you I'm choosing to confide.

Love letters . . . letters of love. What do these words
really mean?

Do they vary within context, left to assumption or
perception or defined by whatever you tell me?

Does it mean I'll always be happy and satisfied? No
challenge will I ever face?

Or does it mean I understand your faults and thoughts
and your shortcomings I learn to embrace.

See, the truth of the matter is that love is a word many
use to say how they feel;

But few pause to think for a second or two about the
actions the word love should reveal.

Few really understand the power that exists between
a woman and a man;
Love is more than a heartfelt conversation or simply
the hold of a hand . . .

See, love means when I hurt, you feel my pain; you do
even more then empathize;
You hold my soul in the palm of your hands and begin
to see through my eyes . . .

See I'm woman, I understand the "definition" of love;
oh please, don't take offense.
My "letters of love" go far beyond words and
combinations of sentences.

See what I want from you is reassurance when my
days are somewhat bleak;
I'm not asking for you to move any mountain for me,
just protect me until I make it to the peak.

Don't feel like you have to drain the ocean for me or
put the stars within my reach,
Or build me a diamond with the tip of your fingers or
let me hang on you like a leech.

But the problem here is the many definitions of love
and the many ways people choose to express it,
the things they do, the actions they take are
individualized among who's expressing it.

That's the tricky part where many fall apart; operating
under totally different definitions,
He's not reaching you, you're not reaching him . . .
what's missing is the connection.

So I'll stop here. Tell him to finish the rest and to make sure the definition is gauged

Because it makes no difference how I may feel about him if he is on a totally different page.

Let me know if you find him . . .

Love,
Real Expectations

POETRY IN MOTION

Love

You know, the Bible talks about what love is—how it's patient, kind, and never boastful. It believes all things and endures all things.

I love the Bible and the Word of God. I haven't experienced that type of love yet. I've given that type of love, but I wonder when it will come my way. I'm being patient, but to be patient means to suffer long.

All I know is this love game is just that—a game. You put your all into someone and get crapped on. It seems like the ones you love don't love you back, and the ones you don't love, love the mess out of you.

I'll be glad when love finally comes my way. I have a lot to give and want to make sure I'm giving it to the right person. I want to give the type of love that when I have a headache, or just don't feel like it, I give anyway because I get pleasure out of knowing my lover is pleased.

The love I have to give is never-ending. Once you're in my heart, you're there forever.

In the Name of Love

In the past people have said love is blind,
but they were wrong about that defining part.
For love is a passionate kind of power
that people choose not to see from their heart.
Love is happiness from inside.
Love should not change as the weather often does.
Even when you argue with the one you love,
you can return to what once was.
Love is a powerful, bold glance at an eagle while he
flies with grace and might without fear in his eyes.
So, in love, I have made my promise true,
In all that I do, I will always do it with you.

Sometimes you just want your significant other to take it all off.

No, I don't mean it quite like you may think.

I would like my special someone to strip for me.

I think you would too.

Sometimes all it takes is a little expression to make everything a lot better.

STRIP FOR ME!
PART I

We met on the job and under the most uncommon of circumstances, poetry in motion some would say.

After a few minutes of innocent communication I knew something had to change,

but could it really be this way?

I wanted to know more about her from what I see, and I realized that maybe she needs something new in her life as she finds her way in a new city, but would I even know what to say?

But her smile hit me in such a way that made me throw caution to the wind, after a few kind words from her lips and the way she laughed at all my jokes, I needed to know how could I get this woman to,

Strip for me.

Strip away all her doubts about a man that she works with, and if he could handle a woman of her elegance, grace, experience, and wealth of knowledge.

Strip away what others might say about two people from two different places and two different times.

Strip away the past hurt that I am sure she has felt from relationships that didn't give to her as much as she gave to them.

Strip away any question of could this man really feel the way he says he does on such short notice?

So I ask, will you Strip for me?

I know her scent and the way she walks, it's intoxicating and surrounds you like a warm hug.

I know the curves of her face, and how her smile reveals the cutest expression ever seen by human eyes.

I want to reinvent the meaning of fun with her, I want to find different ways to please her each and every day

I want her to think of me when the first thought crosses her mind

I want to be that ear when her tongue begins to speak

I want to be that breath of fresh air when stress tries to creep in.

So I ask again, *will you strip for me?*

She told me, "I would like to get to know you too," and for me that struck a chord, creating such a wonderful sound to my soul.

Everything happens for a reason they say, so I have begun to explore the possibility,

Explore the unknown of uncharted territory.

God really put his best foot forward when he blessed me with her presence, the chance for me to know her no matter how strange it came to pass.

So I want you to Strip for me,
Strip for me Mentally
Strip for me in the here and now
Strip for me so I can see inside of you
Strip for me
Just take it all off

Because after last night I have already begun to strip for you!

STRIP FOR ME!
PART II

So the ice is being broken, and we had our first "Kiss," what can I say??

What did I do to deserve such a treat, to be able to gaze in the eyes of such an exquisite woman for an extended period of time?

Getting butterflies in your stomach and having that nervous feeling is overrated, but the moment I saw her face I experienced those feelings like never before.

So the time has approached for me to demonstrate just how into her I really am, giving her my undivided attention and allowing her to come into my world, so that she will feel comfortable and know that it is okay when I ask her to strip for me.

Strip for me because from this moment forward I will put her in a special place even if it's a secret.

Strip for me because I hang on her every word, and I await the next thing she has to say, and I look forward to that "something new" that she will show me about herself.

Her voice, her mannerisms, her style, her overall presentation is second to none. It's almost scary because when I'm around her I feel strong and weak all at the same time.

I feel helpful and helpless all at the same time.

I feel on edge and relaxed at the same time.

Revealing her past to me and what she has been through speaks volumes to my mind. I think to myself who in their right mind would want to hurt her in any way. So I only want her to do one thing and I will take care of the rest, and that's for her to

strip for me....

She is reaching a new level of extreme beauty, with us working side by side each day.

What chapter of her life will unfold next, what new milestones and accomplishments will she tackle? If I can, I would like to be right there to turn the pages with her.

I want to add more laughter to her day
More smiles
More Joy
Even more happiness to her night
More Thoughts
More Passion

I want to eliminate words like hurt, pain, loneliness, stress, and drama from her vocabulary, because as long as I'm around those things wouldn't exist.

There are so many things I want to show her, because even though she is in a situation, we can be in the same place at the same time now. I want her to come to my secret garden; I want her to take a ride on my magic carpet. To places people say they want to go but very seldom are ready to travel.

So Strip for me today and every day

Strip for me because you believe I know what to do even if you don't

Strip for me because right now it feels right

Strip for me because it will happen for a reason as everything does

Strip for me just

Strip for me . . .

Because when it's all said and done we will never be the same

STRIP FOR ME!
PART III

So we decided to take things to the next level. Crossing over to new levels of passion and ecstasy.

What does it all mean? Why me? Why her? Why now?

Are there really answers to these questions, or is the unknown the driving force behind it all?

She is absolutely breathtaking—an amazing ray of sunshine.

I get lost in her eyes and I can't help but to stare at one of God's most precious creations.

There is no denying why I want her to Strip for me . . .

Strip for me, because right now I need someone like you in my life.

Strip for me, because right now you need me too.

She is with another, but her mind is with me. She is with another, but her heart is what I'm after if she lets me.

Forget about the rule book, because the way I feel about her can't be defined by rules.

So Strip for me . . .

Because you should be mine Today, Tomorrow, and Every day.

Strip for me because I promise to take great care of you.

I promise more time for just you,

I promise to take you places you've never been before.

I promise to care more,
To love more,
To love harder,
And I never make promises I can't keep!

You being happy would be an understatement

You having joy would be an understatement

A new word in the English language would have to be created to describe how I would make you feel.

Lately, when I close my eyes I can see her face. When she is not around me, I wonder is she okay?

I wonder does she look at him, like she looks at me?

I wonder is she as playful, does she smile as big, does she laugh as hard?

I ask you to strip for me, because I know you want to

Strip for me, even if you're scared

Strip for me, because I would never hurt you

Strip for me, because what's underneath is the real truth about where you should be.

Strip for me, because when I remove this pen from this pad, I will only be thinking of YOU!!

STRIP FOR ME!
PART IV

Can someone please help me to control my feelings for this woman? It is like something out of a romantic movie.

It's like we have known each other for years or have met somewhere before and didn't know it.

She is amazing. She is what I have been praying for; please don't let this be a dream. She has to be mine, she has to be real, she has to be exactly what I think she is.

If I am right about her then she will strip for me . . .

She knows exactly what to say to make me smile, and hearing her laugh gives me the greatest feeling. I want to give her the world if I could; I want to make all her dreams come true.

I want her to understand that there is such a thing as "True Unconditional love"

I love the woman that she is right now, and the woman she wants to become

I love her attitude about life and how she looks to the future with optimistic eyes

I love it when she calls my name

I love to look in her eyes

I love how this feels even if the moments are short, because she has to leave,

But I hope that one day what are now just moments turn into a lifetime of love.

I knew I wanted her from the first time I said hello, I was ready to change just for her if she asked. So now I ask, will you strip for me???

Strip for me, because what started as a simple "Hi" could end in "I do"

Strip for me because I came to make a difference in your life,

Strip for me because I know what a man is supposed to do

Strip for me because "I want to be your man"

She has such an essence that would make any man weak at the knees

Her lips fit "perfectly" with mine

Her hands fit "perfectly" in mine

Together we look like a "perfect" match

So for this reason I will take "Perfect" care of her heart,

I will be the "perfect" man she has always wanted and I will create a life for us that other people will view as "perfect!"

Will you strip for me so that I can ask you some burning questions that I have?

If so I would ask:

Will you be my friend for life?

Will you be my companion?

Will you be mine?

Will you be my life?

Will you be my wife?

Strip for me so the fun can really begin

Trust in me, trust in my words, and the actions that follow

because once you strip for me, you will uncover Love!

Reflections

2978774

Made in the USA